Children of Divorce in School-Age Care

*A Resource for the School-Age Care
Professional and Youth Care Specialist*

by

Carole D. Weisberg

School-Age NOTES ● Nashville, Tennessee

About the Author

Carole Weisberg is a founding member of the School-Age Directors' Network and the New York State School-Age Care Coalition and has run a large multi-site before-and-after-school program for many years in Westchester County, New York. Throughout her career, Carole has served in many leadership roles in her community and in the State of New York around school-age care issues. She is an accomplished trainer and parent educator and recently received her Masters of Arts in Education from Concordia University.

Since 1995 Carole has been a consultant for New England Counseling and Mediation where she conducts state-mandated parent education classes, titled *Parents are Forever,* for parents who are divorcing or separating.

Carole currently serves as a Program Associate at Yale University's School of the 21st Century (21C), a school-based and school-linked child care and family support system of programs dedicated to the healthy growth and development of all children. She provides technical assistance, training and consultation to 21C Network schools on a variety of implementation issues.

Cover Illustration: A. Michie Shaw

ISBN: 0-917505-11-5

Published by: School-Age NOTES
P.O. Box 40205
Nashville TN 37204

Table of Contents

Acknowledgements

This resource is the outgrowth of a thesis written in fulfillment of the requirements of a Masters of Arts in Education from Concordia University. I wish to acknowledge and thank the professors and facilitators of Concordia University who had the foresight to embark on a groundbreaking endeavor of designing and implementing a Masters Level Program and Curriculum in Education with an emphasis in the field of School-Age Care. As part of this endeavor, it was my privilege to be among an incredible group of intelligent, dynamic and articulate people who are true leaders in the field of School-Age Care.

I also want to thank Resa Fremed and Judy Shapiro who are the guiding forces at New England Counseling and Mediation in Ridgefield, Connecticut and for whom I conduct the parent education course for divorcing couples with children. Their work with families and children of divorce helps countless people through the difficulties of the aftermath of divorce and separation. They provided valuable resources to me as I embarked on this project.

I am also grateful for the lessons learned and the opportunities gained through my experiences as Executive Director of the Lakeland Children's Center.

Finally, I wish to acknowledge the two most important and special people in my life, my children, Jaime and Stephanie. They are my guiding lights.

Preface

S tatistics show a dramatic increase in the number of marriages ending in divorce over the past 40 years, where currently one out of three marriages will end in divorce and approximately 1,000,000 children each year will become children of divorce (National Center for Health Statistics, 1998). These numbers clearly translate into an increase in the number of children attending programs outside of school hours who are experiencing or have experienced their parents' separation and divorce. For the school-age care provider and youth care specialist this presents a great challenge. School-age care providers and youth care specialists are in need of resources and support in terms of knowing and understanding the issues and learning how to deal with situations that arise as a result of divorce and separation. And, although there is a wealth of information on children and divorce, there is little material available that relates directly to the role of the caregiver when faced with the sensitive issues children of divorce can present. The goal of this book is to provide a useful resource to assist the school-age care provider and youth care specialist in understanding, helping and supporting the children and the families with whom they work who have gone through or are presently going through divorce and separation.

The audience for this material is intended for center-based and home-based school-age care providers and youth care specialists, specifically for administrators and head program staff. It is intended for caregivers in a variety of settings who have direct day-to-day contact with school-age children and for administrators who are responsible for training, parent communications and defining program policies and procedures. It is to this audience that I identify with when I refer to "we" and "us" throughout the book. However the material presented will benefit anyone who is in the position of caring for children of any age on a regular basis whose families are going through divorce or separation.

My 17 years experience as an administrator in the school-age care field and five years experience conducting Parent Education programs for separating and divorcing parents, has led me to believe that there is a need for resources on children and divorce for school-age care providers and youth care specialists that is specific to our role in the lives of the children and families we serve. Having also conducted staff training and presented workshops on this topic at several conferences for school-age care program staff, I find that many programs are dealing with issues around divorce on many levels. For example, at one such training I conducted a participant asked how does one respond when parents who are newly single start acting like teenagers as they begin dating again? One can see that it is not only the children's behaviors and feelings that present challenges, but very often it is the parents' behaviors that can cause the biggest concerns.

Although there are many excellent resources available on divorce and separation, there is a lack of materials and resources that speaks directly to the role of child care staff who are faced with an increasing number of children of divorce in their programs and family day care homes. One resource, which is considered the standard reference on the topic, is *Surviving the Breakup: How Children and Parents Cope with Divorce* by Judith Wallerstein and Joan Kelly (1980). This book represents the first major study on the immediate and long-term effects of divorce and has had a major impact on legal issues surrounding children and divorce and subsequent writings on the topic. However, even though there is much material on the topic itself, there is little reference to the roles of non-relatives and caregivers. And, on a personal level, as the mother of two children who has gone through separation and divorce myself, I know how much support I and my children needed then, and yet I was not always able to seek it out or know exactly where to find it. In many instances I find myself thinking, "If I only knew then what I know now..." Therefore, it is my hope that this resource will not only be helpful to the professional caregivers who work with families going through these experiences, but also, and subsequently, will be a benefit to the children and their parents as well.

Chapter One:
Introduction

The nature of the changing family has long been a topic of concern for children. The image of the two-parent nuclear family where father is the breadwinner and mother is at home caring for the children is quickly fading and, in fact, very rarely exists in today's world. The norm has shifted to families where both parents are working outside the home and the majority of children are being cared for by non-relatives. As Elkind states in *The Ties That Stress* (1994):

> *Childcare by paid professionals is rapidly becoming the national norm, as large numbers of women with children under school-age enter the full-time workforce. Single-parent families have become the fastest growing family structure in America in the 1990s, as more and more parents choose divorce over marital dissatisfaction…. Blended families, consisting of stepsiblings and half-siblings from two and sometimes three marriages, are not unusual. (p. 3)*

The rising rate of divorce, single parent households, remarriages and blended families have repercussions which effect not only the children and their families, but also all the other people involved in the child's life. School-age care providers and youth care specialists who are or have been involved with children and families of divorce are well aware of how these changes in children's lives effect the children as well as the caregivers themselves.

Historically, couples who may have considered themselves in bad marriages stayed together for many reasons including, but not limited to: social convention, financial concerns and, most often, "for the sake of the children" (Baris & Garrity, 1988). Since the early 1970's and the adoption of a system of "no-fault" divorce across all 50 states, it has become increasingly easier and more socially acceptable to divorce. No longer were couples staying together "for the sake of the children." In fact, conventional thinking had shifted and perpetuated a myth

> *…that children were resilient, that if parents felt fulfilled in pursuing what they felt were their individual goals, then the children, in turn, would benefit from the parents overall improvement. In essence, the "Me" generation philosophy was introduced into the family.*
> *(Baris & Garrity 1988, p. 1)*

The National Center for Health Statistics (1994 & 1995) and Bradburn-Stern (1990) suggests that 70% of all children born since 1990 will spend time in a single parent family. The statistics show that 60% of divorces occur for people between the ages of 25-39 (the child bearing and rearing years) and approximately 1,000,000 children each year become children of divorce. These changes in family life style and parenting arrangements are causing complex problems for schools and child care providers (Keller, 1997).

> *Principals [in the schools] and others who must juggle family concerns with legal requirements and practical matters say they are not getting much guidance from the relatively scattered laws on the subject or from experts.*
> *(Keller, 1997, p.1)*

Unfortunately, for the child care community, and in particular the school-age care community, there is little support for the caregiver or information available to them that is specific to their roles to help them navigate through these complex issues. As more and more parents rely on the schools and caregivers for support, those who care for their children are under increasing pressure to know more about the issues in order to best serve the needs of the children and families with whom they work.

Increasingly, educators and child care providers find themselves in the middle of the parents' conflict. Therefore, they not only have to cope with the resulting effects on the child of their parents' separation and divorce, but often have to deal with parents who want caregivers to take sides in the battle. "Conflict is the chief danger to children of divorce" (Waldron, 1995, p. 68). Parents who can each maintain a positive relationship and regular contact with their children, can manage their own conflict through the divorce process, are civil with one another and can co-parent successfully, will find that their children will be better able to cope themselves and have fewer negative effects from their parents' separation and divorce.

> *The research on long term effects of divorce on children seem to indicate that when the level of conflict is controlled for and the custodial arrangements are appropriate to the needs of the children, there are no differences between children of divorce and children of intact families on: moral development; social development; academic performance; psychopathology levels; and self-concept. (Waldron 1995, p.53)*

This is important for those who work with children of divorce and have regular contact with their parents to know. After one training, a young participant expressed how well she had fared through her parents' divorce. She related how everyone gets along, her parents remain friends, each has remarried and all can get together for significant family events that support the children. Her story illustrates how her parents' ability to get along kept her from experiencing negative effects from her parents' separation and divorce.

Sadly, it is not always the case that parents are able to behave in a civil or cooperative manner with one another. Parents are often so consumed by their own emotions and conflicts that they lose sight of the needs of their children.

> *The research evidence suggests that it is not the effects of divorce itself that have negative effects on children's behavior, but the conflict between parents that predates and accompanies divorce. (Grusec & Lytton, 1988, p. 431)*

In fact, a common effect of divorce for many adults is a diminished capacity to parent.

> *Adding significantly to the widespread distress of the children is the fact that many of them face the tensions and sorrows of divorce with little help from their parent, or anyone else, for during the critical months following the separation parental care often diminishes, not because parents are necessarily less loving or less concerned with their children during divorce, but because the radical alterations in their lives tend to focus their attention on their own troubles. (Wallerstein & Kelly, 1980, p. 36)*

In today's society, many families live far from their own extended families, they move frequently (on average of every two to three years), are working longer hours, and find themselves isolated within their own communities and neighborhoods. Elkind (1994) calls this the "postmodern permeable family" which has resulted in a "new family imbalance." This isolation has created an ever increasing need for families to connect somewhere, especially where their children are concerned, and most certainly for families experiencing separation and divorce. Many parents just don't know where to turn. When parents turn to their school-age care provider for guidance and support, it would serve one well to not only be sensitive to their needs, but to be as well informed as one can. This also means knowing when and where to refer parents to other professionals or agencies that can better address their needs.

The effect of diminished parenting for children of divorce, the difficulty of many parents to cope with the stresses and conflicts of their everyday lives coupled with the added stress of divorce and separation places a greater need for school-age care providers to fulfill the role of "extended family" and to provide a safe place for children where there is consistency of care and adults with whom they can form meaningful relationships.

We may ask ourselves, then, what is the role of the school-age practitioner? It has been suggested that school-age programs may very well be the "new" extended family. *School-Age Care Providers: Extended Day or Extended Family? - A staff development book*, (Ollhoff & Ollhoff, 1996) states that, "When we take care of children, we are in an extended family role. In fact, we are serving the whole family when we take care of the children" (p. 9). Over the course of time parents, whether divorced or not, have come to rely on many school-age care providers to take on the role of extended family. Kendall (1981) observed that changing family structures and child-rearing patterns have altered, and suggests that since traditional sources of support for families with children are not readily available, new or additional support systems for families must be found. Certainly, the school-age care program is among the "new or additional support systems" on whom families have come to rely.

This may sound like a tall order for the school-age care professional. However, meeting the social and emotional needs of the children and providing a healthy atmosphere for them are the most important roles of school-age care. In order to meet this challenge, it is hoped that this book will provide a source of information as well as guidelines to meet various situations that may arise regarding the children, their parents and the other significant adults who may be involved in the child's life and the program.

It is important to remember that we walk a fine line in the lives of the children in our care. We are not their school teachers or psychological counselors, we are not their parents or relatives, even though we are often asked for advice and guidance by parents. We may be asked to handle many situations that were once handled in the home, such as overseeing homework and guiding behavior. However, we must always remember that it is not our role to be a surrogate parent to the child - but to be a support to the parent and the family.

The material presented here is designed to be a source of information and a resource to the school-age care provider and youth care specialist on the issues of children and divorce. The following chapters will cover a review of the literature on the effects of divorce and separation on children and parents, and a discussion of the role of the school-age care provider and youth care specialist. To supplement this discussion, I corresponded with school-age care professionals throughout the United States in order to include some actual experiences others are facing on the issues involving children and divorce. The experiences of others along with my own experiences are included for anecdotal purposes only, designed to provide some real-life situations to illustrate the many issues that program staff are facing. Included as well will be a discussion on how we, as the new extended family, can have an impact on minimizing the negative effects of divorce on the children and families we serve. And, finally, a specific set of practices will be suggested which SAC professionals and youth care specialists will, hopefully, find useful and which can be implemented in their own programs.

Chapter Two:
Effects of Divorce on Families

Children are the innocent victims of divorce.
(Adler & Archambault, 1990)

It is clear that divorce and separation are now a part of many school-age children's lives, the effects of which are carried with them throughout their days. This chapter will provide an overview of the effects of divorce on children and families. Through a review of the literature a greater understanding of the underlying feelings behind the behaviors can be gained and, therefore, insights learned for the school-age care providers and youth care specialists who are dealing with these issues.

General reactions of children and parents to divorce:

Once the decision to divorce is made and the words spoken, thus begins a time of emotional upheaval and turmoil for the family. According to Waldron (1995) the first year of a divorce is dominated by feelings of confusion, guilt, shame and anger for all involved, both children and parents. In *Crazy Time: Surviving Divorce*, Abigail Trafford (1982) explains that, for adults, during the first year or two following separation, "It's a time when... emotions take on a life of their own.... You are not yourself.... Yet this is usually the very painful transition period [one has] to go through before [one] can establish a new life.... It's equivalent to the mourning period after death and catastrophe" (p. 43). Waldron further states that, "Although the dominant emotion in a separation appears to be anger, the most important underlying feeling is loss. There are many losses that occur when two people who have been together for a while separate..." (p. 16). For parents, it is the loss of the marriage itself. Gone are the hopes and dreams of what the marriage was to be, their social situation changes; friends may be lost and extended family may be far away or in some cases, may even turn away; finances are a concern; the house may have to be sold; and there is loss of the children, or at least, time with the children (Waldron, 1995).

Children were heavily burdened by their enormous sense of loss. ...Older children and adolescents were preoccupied with the loss of the family as an ongoing presence, with the lost sense of continuity and structure the family had provided in their lives (Wallerstein & Kelly, 1980, p. 46).

This is especially true for the younger school-age child, as is further illustrated in the observation that, "...the most striking response among six- to eight-year-old children was their pervasive sadness" (p. 65).

These reactions to the divorce and separation are called grief. Both the children and their parents are mourning the marriage. There is, however, added difficulty for children who are grieving the marriage as Vicki Lansky's *Divorce Book for Parents: Helping Your Children Cope with Divorce and Its Aftermath* (1989) points out "...in death, mourning is accepted and encouraged, and friends and relatives are usually available to help and console both adults and children. But in the crisis of divorce, the support of family and parents is usually not available to children" (p. 29). Parents, themselves, may not always have support available either. In my experience with participants in parent education classes I often find that following the decision to divorce many parents throw themselves into their work or their children or both. They need to be reminded to take care of themselves, take time for themselves and seek support for themselves. Friends and relatives alone may not always be the best source of support. They may take sides and in trying to be helpful only support what the parent says, never challenging or questioning decisions, or worse they may "fuel the fires" by urging combative behaviors. Without good support, parents, too, are left to fend for themselves while grieving the marriage.

Mourning the Marriage

Families going through divorce and separation mourn the marriage and experience similar reactions to people mourning a death. Elisabeth Kubler-Ross (1969) identified five stages terminally-ill patients and their families go through when dealing with illness and the prognosis of death. The stages are: denial and isolation, anger and resentment, bargaining, depression (stemming from guilt, shame and a profound sense of loss), and, finally, acceptance. Of course, there are some significant differences between mourning a death and mourning a marriage. For example, participants in my parent education classes have stated that the death of a spouse must be easier to come to terms with. They feel that divorce is worse, especially if there are children, because then they must continue to be in each other's lives and there is seemingly no end to their involvement. This is especially troublesome and stressful when the relationship between the divorcing couple is filled with anger, resentment, distrust and hostility. Additionally, reactions to the divorce are not necessarily sequential, and, not all members of the family will be at the same stage at the same time. For instance, Mom may be depressed, Dad angry and the

NORMAL REACTIONS

(*Mourning the Marriage*)

In Children

In Children & Parents

❖ Health/Sleep Changes

❖ Denial

❖ Regression

❖ Anger

❖ Insecurity

❖ Bargaining

❖ Guilt/Self Blame

❖ Sadness/Depression

❖ Protective of Parents

❖ Acceptance

children stuck in denial wishing their parents would get back together. Or Dad might be in denial, Mom angry, one child resentful and the other depressed. In fact, it is probably more likely that each individual member of the family is experiencing the separation differently. Research supports the difficulty parents have in terms of awareness of the needs of their children, especially when they are struggling with their own reactions to the divorce (Wallerstein & Kelly, 1980).

> *A prominent family in the community was going through a divorce and their middle school-age child was in my program. It was painful to see what they were going through but each family member was in a different place with these changes. The mother was very strong, seemingly unaffected. The father was devastated. The child … was numb.*
>
> (as related by a school-age program director)

These, then are the general reactions to the divorce that most people experience in their own unique ways. Mourning the marriage takes time, and for those who work with children in school-age care, it takes patience, too. There are general factors that impact children's reactions to parental separation. Some factors will have a positive impact and others will have negative consequences.

General factors that impact children's reactions:

Children's reactions to their parents' divorce are dependent on a number of factors. While each child is unique, these factors coupled with a child's own temperament, inner resources and ability to handle change will influence their reactions. According to the literature (Bradburn-Stern, 1990, Marston, 1994 and Wallerstein & Kelly, 1980), the following will impact how children react:

- ❖ the number of adjustments children have to make
- ❖ the chaos of the first year of the divorce
- ❖ the degree of change in the child's image of their parents
- ❖ the child's ability or inability to understand the divorce
- ❖ the child's own personality assets or deficits
- ❖ the child's reaction and adjustment when parents begin to meet adults away from the family
- ❖ the consistency and quality of contact with the non-residential parent
- ❖ the availability of a supportive network
- ❖ the ability of parents to move beyond anger and conflict to begin cooperative parenting

The **number of adjustments** children have to make impacts their reaction to the divorce. For a child in the midst of the emotions of parental separation having to move only adds to the trauma. A new school, new neighborhood, and the prospect of having to make new friends can be very difficult. Not only is this difficult in terms of a fear of the unknown, but would also add to the number of losses the child would be experiencing, i.e. loss of the familiarity and security of their school surrounding, their neighborhood and, more importantly, loss of their friends. For some their standard of living changes. They may have to move from a large house to a smaller one or from a house to an apartment complex. Clearly, the fewer disruptions in a child's life in relation to these adjustments the better it is for the child.

The **chaos of the first year** impacts the child's reaction to the divorce. As previously stated, a common early result of the divorce is diminished parenting which can add to adjustment problems. "In addition to the emotional remoteness of the parents and high visibility of the marital conflict, children also experience the diminished amount of time their parents had available to them" (Wallerstein & Kelly, 1980, p. 42).

The **degree of change in the child's image of their parents** who they have counted on for protection and nurturance impacts their reactions to the divorce. Children experience a "heightened sense of their own vulnerability" and children begin to see their parents as vulnerable. This coupled with the "emotional remoteness" of their parents can have a negative effect on their reactions.

Children of all ages will experience fear, sadness, anger, anxiety, etc., yet at different stages some of these feelings are more pronounced due to the **child's ability (or inability) to understand**. These reactions are common, however, the duration and degree to which they impact the child's reaction will relate to the child's stage of development and their understanding of the events happening around them.

The **child's own personality assets or deficits** will impact their reactions. Children's temperament, psychological health, degree of social skills competency and self-image will help or hinder their ability to cope. "Of those children who had been in good psychological health prior to the divorce, those who had been functioning adequately, and those remaining who had been burdened by repeated failures in various aspects of their lives, all responded differently" (Wallerstein & Kelly, 1980, p. 52).

When **parents begin to meet adult needs away from family**, it is often hard for children to understand. Often, during unhappy marriages and following divorce and separation, a child and one parent may have formed a very close relationship. When a parent takes on a lover or other adult interests, the child may feel rejected and lonely, and abandoned once again. Eventually this situation can work out to be better for both the parent and the child, but initial reaction and adjustment can be disruptive and disorienting for the child.

Consistency and quality of contact from the non-residential parent is a factor in how children will be effected by the divorce. Children of all ages who were able to maintain a close stable relationship with both the custodial and non-custodial parent were identified as having good ego functioning, adequate or high self-esteem and no depression. The importance of the father-child relationship was especially significant for school-age children between nine and twelve, or entering adolescence. They took intense pleasure in visiting with their father. Conversely, when visits were irregular or infrequent and the father was generally unreliable or absent the resulting negative effects on the child included lower self-esteem and feeling rejected, rebuffed, unloved and unlovable.

The **availability of a supportive network** helps to foster positive effects of divorce on children and families. During the difficult transitions and changes that divorce presents, the availability of family and friends that offer positive support is invaluable. However, as previously noted family and friends may not always be the best support and seeking professional support may be needed for both children and parents. This can be found either through counseling, support groups or other community agencies. And the school-age care provider and youth care specialist are included in the network of support that a family may come to rely upon.

The **ability of parents to move past anger and conflicts** to begin or resume cooperative parenting may be the most important step in positively effecting children's ability to cope with divorce. Children need to be able to love both parents and have free and open access to each parent unencumbered or hindered emotionally or physically by the other parent. As mentioned above, all children who were able to maintain close and stable relationships with both their parents showed no signs of depression, maintained positive social development, had good self-esteem and were more likely to be in good psychological health.

Central themes of children's responses to divorce and separation:

In addition to the above factors that impact children's reaction to divorce, there is a range of feelings and concerns that were found to be common in children from the very youngest through those in their adolescent years. "Psychologists agree that the divorce process is always traumatic for children, at least temporarily and sometimes permanently" (Adler & Archambault, 1990).

According to Wallerstein & Kelly (1980) the following central themes were common experiences for children:

● **Divorce is frightening:** Children "experienced a heightened sense of their own vulnerability…. They confronted a world which suddenly appeared to have become less reliable, less predictable, and less likely in their view to provide for their needs and expectations" (p. 45).

● **Divorce is a time of sadness and yearning:** Children mourned the familiarity, continuity and stability of the family structure. They felt an enormous sense of loss. They were teary, moody and sad. Many children exhibited signs of acute depression. One child, whose parents were involved in a highly divisive and contentious divorce, would crawl on the floor and call himself a lowly snake. He felt so bad that he would try to climb into the garbage can. He stated that he wanted to throw himself away.

● **Divorce is a time of worry:** Children worried whether they would see the absent or non-custodial parent again. And, they worried about the absent parent. Where does Daddy live? Who will be his friends? And, who was taking care of Daddy?

> *One child in our program was visibly upset about her parents' divorce and we suspected depression. During a "wishing tree" activity, the children were asked to make a wish and this child pinned her wish for "a dad" on our wishing tree.*
>
> (related by a program director)

Children are aware of their parents' anger even though they may not understand it completely, and worry that if one parent wins the battle, the other parent could be banished from the household forever and they would never see that parent again. "Many children were concerned over one or both parents'" emotional stability and their capacity to manage without the other's help" (p. 47). Many worried intensely about their mothers, too. They worried about the health and well-being of the remaining parent and worried if they would be left without any parents at all.

Children also worried about changes in their financial and social situations. "They were concerned about money, about changing schools, about moving to another house and neighborhood. And, as parents acquired new friends, lovers, and fiancés, the children worried about being displaced by the new relationships…and of being forgotten in the shuffle" (p. 48).

● **Divorce is a time of feeling rejected:** Children felt rejected by their parents. The combined effects of their parents' preoccupation with their own problems, the diminishment of parental involvement and parenting skills left children feeling as if no one cared about them. Young children felt especially rejected by the departing parent as they did not understand the dynamics of one spouse leaving another as different from their leaving them. Some of the children, especially the boys, identified with the departed father and felt acutely their mother's anger and criticism for the father as if it were directed at them. For school-age children, six- to twelve-year-old boys felt the most rejected by their fathers.

● **Divorce is a lonely time:** "The loneliness of the child at this time is profound. …The child feels that both his parents are slipping out of his life…one or both parents appears preoccupied or behaves in unfamiliar ways" (p. 48). The intense loneliness of the children could be related to the sense of rejection they felt and to their yearning for the departed parent. One way in which children attempt to stave off the acute pain of loss they are feeling is to cling to fantasies of their parents reuniting. Most children wish for and long for their parents to get back together. As parents, we may not always see this happening. In my own situation, I didn't think that my children harbored this longing. They were older and seemed to have accepted the divorce and to be handling things pretty well. However, upon reflection, I remember that the months following the separation - after their father had moved out of the house - they were watching a particular movie we had on tape over and over again. The movie was the original version of "The Parent Trap." The plot of this movie is about twin sisters who were separated from each other when their parents divorced, one living with her mother and the other living with her father. They eventually meet one summer and the remainder of the movie is spent on their efforts to get their parents back together. They succeed, of course. It is, after all, a movie.

● **Divorce is a time of conflicting loyalties:** Children feel drawn into their parents' battle. "They feel pulled by love and loyalty in both directions. ...School-age children particularly appeared to conceptualize the divorce as a struggle in which each participant demanded one's primary loyalty, and this conception greatly increased the conflict and unhappiness of the child" (p. 49). Children are placed in a no-win situation when this happens. If they move in the direction of one parent, it was felt as if they were betraying the other parent, which was sometimes confirmed by the actions of the other parent. "Their conflict of loyalty placed them in a solitary position midway in the marital struggle. ...Some youngsters resolved this unbearable dilemma by joining the battle in alignment with one parent, in bitter anger against the other" (p. 49).

● **Divorce is a time of anger:** All children, regardless of age, experienced a rise in aggression. "...There was a significant rise across the board in general crankiness and rebelliousness" (p. 50).

> *Two children, nine and eleven years, who were siblings...in our SAC program... had recently been through a divorce. [The] children fought with each other and were aggressive toward other children.*
> (related by a program director)

Some of these behaviors are in response to the parental anger and fighting they may have witnessed. But, children also felt that the divorce was an act of selfishness on the part of their parents without consideration of their needs. Children wanted to know, "Why me?" "What did I do to deserve this?" Children who feel this way may bring their negative feelings into the SAC program.

[A ten-year-old girl in the program]...a person who normally is very easy-going, now began to act out. She started disagreeing with many things that were brought up at our program meetings. She had a very negative opinion about almost everything. She...became cynical."

(related by a SAC director)

● **Feelings of Guilt:** The researchers found that, contrary to the prevailing belief, not all children feel responsible for the disruption of the family. However, very young children, under age eight, are more likely to feel as if they caused their parents' break-up. Older children who were more likely to feel responsible for their parents' divorce "were more often troubled in other ways and had symptoms which also reflected difficulties in other parts of their adjustment" (p. 50). Parents should always reassure their children that the divorce is not their fault. Kids think like kids, they wonder if they said something or did something that caused one parent to leave or one parent to get angry with the other parent. They may think that because they didn't clean up their room when asked, or that their school teacher called because of some mishap at school or homework wasn't done correctly or wasn't done at all that they may somehow be responsible for their parents' divorce.

Responses to Divorce Within Children's Age Groupings and Developmental Stage:

The above general factors impact children of all ages. However, there are reactions that are similar for children within certain age groupings and developmental stages. For school-age children this breaks down to two age groupings: ages six to eight and and ages nine to twelve.

Six Years to Eight Years:

The hallmark emotional task of six to eight year olds is their active participation in a process of branching out from the family. This is the stage during which children begin the transition away from home into relationships with friends, hobbies, activities, and the school environment. ...Six- to eight-year-old children are building a sense of mastery and sense of self-esteem by relating to others through friendships and activities. This is a crucial age for sex role identification and for the building of confidence and self-esteem. (Baris & Garrity, 1988, p. 35)

WHAT KIDS NEED TO DO

❖ Overcome sense of:
Rejection
Humiliation
Unloveableness
Powerlessness

❖ Resolve Anger

❖ Stop Blaming

❖ Disengage from the Parental Conflict

❖ Accept Reality & Permanence

❖ Preserve Ideals of Love and Loyalty

Early elementary school-age children whose parents are divorcing are frequently preoccupied with feelings of sadness, loss, rejection and guilt. "For children of six to eight a divorce is all too real and painful. These children have a sufficient awareness of the larger outside world to know what divorce means…" (Baris & Garrity, 1988, p. 37). They often become absorbed by fears of rejection and abandonment. Children are deeply concerned that they will lose the non-custodial parent. They worry that another child in their parent's life will replace them. Children this age rely on their parents for stability. After the divorce they tend to feel insecure and fearful. They feel they are being divorced or rejected. Youngest children are still caught up in "magical thinking" so they cling to reuniting or rescuing fantasies. Belief in superheroes impacts their self-esteem when they cannot rescue or reunite. Because they are feeling powerless, taking on the persona of a superhero allows them to feel powerful and in control. Older children within this age range are too old to escape into fantasy and too young to understand fully that they are not responsible for the divorce.

Children at these ages may (Marston, 1994):

❖ cry easily, get cranky or anxious.

❖ become clingy and have difficulty separating from parents at school.

❖ regress to an earlier stage.

❖ be very angry about the divorce and may turn their anger toward themselves, becoming depressed or withdrawn.

❖ experience poor concentration, become easily distracted; school performance may suffer.

❖ experience stress related headaches or stomachaches.

❖ take out anger on custodial parent who is a safe, convenient target.

❖ have strong hopes for reconciliation and actively seek to reunite their parents (sometimes by creating problems that force parental involvement).

Children at this age can be extremely angry. This anger may be acted out or turned into shame, or self-blame. Worry about their parents or their own well being is very common at this age. This worry may be expressed by fear of not being picked up on time by either parent or by having difficulty going to sleep (Marston, 1994). The school-age care provider and youth care specialist have most likely seen all of these behaviors acted out in their before-and-after-school programs.

Children of this age commonly resort to trickery, illness or accidents in an effort to bring their parents together again. The scheme individual children use is often dictated by what they have seen work in the past.

*Becoming hurt or sick is one of the most effective tools in all families
to unite parents through worry and tragedy.*
                                                    (Baris & Garrity, 1988,p. 37)

Nine Years to 12 Years:

Research shows a noticeable difference between younger school-age children
and children from age nine to twelve years in their response to divorce. It is worth
noting that Wallerstein & Kelly (1980) were taken by surprise at this finding "because psychological theory does not suggest a significant distinction between
children in the primary grades and those in the fourth or fifth grades" (p. 71). For
school-age care providers who work with children from five or six years to twelve
years of age, often in multi-age settings, this finding comes as no surprise. School-
age care providers have long observed significant differences in the younger children in grades K-3 from those in grades 4-6 (the preteen years).

> *Developmentally, nine- to twelve-year-olds are focused on establishing
> proficiency in areas they began to master during earlier stages. These
> areas include peer relationships as well as athletic, academic, and artistic
> pursuits. Nine- to twelve-year-olds are idealistic and enjoy the pride of
> being able to make genuine contributions to their community through
> participation in service organizations, church-related activities, and school
> extracurricular activities. ... By nine to twelve years of age, children
> are able to participate fully in discussions. They have a vastly improved
> grasp of adult issues including those surrounding their parents' divorce.*
>   *(Baris & Garrity, 1988, pp. 47-48)*

Wallerstein & Kelly found that the children in their study experienced rapid
growth and strengthening of ego from the eighth to ninth year. They found many of
the children from nine- to twelve-years-old "had presence, poise and courage....
These youngsters ... were actively struggling to master a host of conflicting feelings and fears, and trying to give coherence and continuity to the baffling disorder
in which they now found themselves" (pp. 71-72).

> *Children nine to twelve years of age...characteristically express a
> great deal of empathic understanding of their parents' attitudes and
> reasons for the divorce. They demand to know...why the divorce has
> taken place, and how they will be affected by resultant changes. The
> capacity for understanding also serves to heighten their awareness of
> their own vulnerability.*   *(Baris & Garrity, 1988, p. 48)*

Children in this age group tend to feel alone and frightened, but because they are easily embarrassed they pretend to act cool and unaffected. "Moreover, nine- to twelve-year-olds are characterized by their idealism. ...In the divorce situation, their idealism easily can produce a sense of rage" (Baris & Garrity, 1988, p. 48). Kids at this age have a strong sense of loyalty and tend to side with the parent who they feel was "wronged." They are susceptible to enter into an alignment with one parent against the other. They tend to see the world in absolutes (black or white, right or wrong, good or bad). However, children of this age can be extremely angry with both parents for the divorce. They are struggling to define their identity and experience confusion due to their parental separation. They may feel threatened by the possibility of losing their friends or changing schools...this is the age of self-consciousness.

Children at this age may (Marston, 1994):

  ❖ suffer sadness, loneliness, insecurity and feelings of helplessness.

  ❖ experience intense, well organized and clearly object-oriented anger at one or both parents.

  ❖ engage in stealing, lying or refusing to go to school.

  ❖ prematurely become involved with dating and early sexual behavior.

  ❖ experience school performance problems.

  ❖ assume the role of the absent parent to support and comfort the custodial parent.

The effects of divorce on children are related to many factors. The child's own inner resources and ability to cope, coupled with the number of changes in their lives, the continuity and involvement of the child with the absent parent (usually the father) are all important factors. But, the most important factor is the behaviors of their parents and their parents' ability to cope with the divorce themselves, and resume normal parenting of their children (Waldron, 1995).

Warning Signs In Children

❖ An exaggeration in the normal responses

❖ Frequent nightmares

❖ Intense, unrealistic fears

❖ Ongoing health complaints

   (i.e., headache, stomachaches, diarrhea, constipation)

❖ Extended changes in sleeping or eating habits

❖ Preoccupation with illness in self and/or others

❖ School troubles, lying, stealing

❖ Explosive behavior

❖ Accident proneness

❖ Verbalizing despair

❖ Giving away their possessions

❖ Withdrawing to the point of isolation

❖ Significant weight loss or gain

❖ Destroying own or other's property

❖ Deliberately hurting or wounding themselves

❖ Significant change in personality

❖ Refusing to stay with formerly trusted adults

❖ Running away from home or child care setting

Chapter Three:
Red Flags
and Warning Signs

With the increasing numbers of children of divorce in out-of-school-time care, school-age care providers and youth care specialists need to be sensitive to all the varied effects of divorce on children in order to adequately meet their needs. Recognizing the warning signs in children when normal reactions are exaggerated and behaviors fall outside the norm is crucial in order to know when children and families need to seek professional assistance. It is equally important that caregivers become knowledgeable about and aware of the issues that parents are dealing with and the common mistakes that they make which can have devastating effects on their children.

The normal reactions to divorce, as discussed in Chapter Two, are likened to that of grief and mourning a death. There is denial, fear, sadness, depression, and anger for both the children and their parents. Children may experience changes in their health and sleep patterns; regress to an earlier developmental stage for comfort; children will feel insecure; some may feel guilty and blame themselves for their parents' break-up; and children become protective of their parents. Some children are acutely embarrassed by their parents' divorce and may shy away from talking about it at all. These reactions are normal and first appear during the initial period of separation and can usually last for about one year (Bradburn-Stern 1990, Waldron 1995, Wallerstein & Kelly 1980). There is cause for concern when these normal reactions are exaggerated or last well beyond the initial year when the divorce process is settled and new routines are underway.

There are distinct warning signs in children of divorce which school-age care providers and youth care specialists should become aware.

Warning Signs in Children of Divorce

The warning signs in children encompass a range of behaviors from severe depression and withdrawal to acting out and explosive behaviors. Although each child is unique and reacts in their own way, the following behaviors are cause for concern, especially if they are ongoing and excessive. They are evidenced by frequent nightmares and intense unrealistic fears; health complaints such as head-ache, stomachache, diarrhea or constipation; a preoccupation with illness in them-selves and in others; a change in eating habits and/or significant weight loss. Se-verely depressed children may verbalize despair, wishing their parents had never been married, wishing that they had never been born. Some children may withdraw to the point of isolation. They may give away their possessions, destroy their own or other's property. Children who are depressed may hurt or wound themselves and may become accident-prone. Any significant change in a child's personality is cause for concern.

Additionally, some children become intensely angry. Anger, belligerence and contrariness, for many, is a way to avoid dealing with other underlying feelings that may be overwhelming, such as the feelings of abandonment and of loss. Children may have trouble in school with peers, teachers and other adults. They may start lying and stealing. Some children may refuse to stay with formerly trusted adults and some run away from home or the child care setting. During one training a participant shared a story about a ten-year-old boy in her program whose parents were in the midst of divorcing. It seems that he would "confess" to stealing or some other mishap, such as hitting another child, to his mother almost every evening when she picked him up. What baffled the school-age care provider was that he had done none of these things during the day; he had been confessing to other children's behaviors or fabricating the misbehavior all together. There could have been several reasons for this kind of behavior; any one of the following may have been at play: due to diminished parenting, the child may have needed his mother's attention so badly that he would manufacture reasons for her to focus on him or, longing for the return of the security of his intact family, he might have felt that he could bring his parents back together by creating reasons for them to jointly be concerned about him. He may have had guilt feelings for the break-up of his parents' marriage and might have actually felt responsible for the misbehaviors of others.   In any event, and whatever the cause, this child was clearly in need of some outside intervention to help him sort out the feelings and behaviors with which he was dealing.

As outlined in Chapter Two, several factors impact the reactions of children to their parents' divorce. The child's own inner resources are certainly a significant factor. However, the single most important factor impacting the child is the behav-ior of their parents. This is probably the area in which school-age care providers and youth care specialists find the most problematic. Parents caught in their own conflict are grieving the marriage as well. Unfortunately, they can lose sight of the needs of their children largely because they are so needy themselves (Wallerstein & Kelly, 1980).

> *I had a girl aged nine years who had been in my program for four years. Her parents went through a very unhappy, quarrelsome divorce. Their behaviors greatly affected this young girl. She became very unhappy, belligerent and a big problem in dealing with her peers in our program. I had to relate some of these experiences to the girl's mother. This parent needed a lot of guidance as to what direction she should take. She finally sought professional counseling and learned slowly how to deal with her daughter.*
>
> (related by a SAC provider)

There are some common mistakes parents make which can have repercussions for their children and repercussions, as well, for the people who care for their children, especially the school-age care provider and youth care specialist. The following will outline the common mistakes that parents make. Recognizing these signs will be valuable in order to offer help to the parents in the form of constructive suggestions or sensitive referrals for outside professional assistance.

Common Mistakes Parents Make

Parents become less available to their children emotionally and physically. Parenting skills diminish and children may be left on their own to figure out what is happening and why (Wallerstein & Kelly, 1980). Parents may "tragedize" the divorce to their children and, therefore, set them up for negative consequences. "The increase in aggressive behavior often seen, for example, will in some instances not be from the divorce per se, but from the failure of the parents to continue to follow routines and set limits..." (Waldron, 1995, p. 48).

Some parents start to rely on their children for emotional support and some expect them to take on more responsibilities, including adult responsibilities, than were previously required of them. This is called *parentification*. According to Waldron, "Parentification is essentially the process whereby burdens and responsibilities that ordinarily fall on the shoulders of adults end up on the children" (p. 49). Sometimes it is not the parents who act in this manner, but the child who decides it's up to them to take on the parental role. This is especially true for older siblings and children in the eight- to twelve-year-old range. One director of a remedial after-school program described a ten-year-old who was one of four children in a family experiencing divorce, and although not the oldest, he was the oldest boy, "The ten-year-old brother has assumed the role of 'father'. He has become bossy, mouthy, and over-protective of the others. He believes his mother doesn't deserve respect from him because he does everything around the house now...."

The "Don'ts"
Mistakes Parents Make

❖ Sending messages through the children to each other

❖ Asking children to keep secrets from the other parent

❖ Using children as pawns in the power struggle

❖ Belittle and criticize the other parent in front of the children

❖ Telling their children what to think and feel

❖ Asking children to take sides

❖ Become less available to their children emotionally and physically

❖ Pumping their children for information about their ex-spouse

❖ Use children as confidants

❖ Comparing their feelings about their ex or the divorce to those their children have

❖ Putting children in the middle of the parents' conflict

❖ Relying on their children as a source for their own emotional support

Parents who are unable to communicate with each other, make the mistake of using their children as go-betweens and send messages to each other through the children (Waldron, 1995). This places children squarely in the middle of the parents' conflict. Even if the messages are seemingly innocent or just out of convenience, they have the potential for putting children in uncomfortable situations. This can be in the form of asking children to give instructions to the other parent or asking for responses to questions, i.e. "Tell your father this..." or "Ask your mother that..." or it can be in the form of giving children written communications to give to the other parent. One participant in my parent education class reported that when dropping off his child between visitations he would send her in with the child support payments and sometimes other communications to give to her mother. It was clear by his body language, tone of voice and a few comments he made that he sorely resented making these payments to his ex-spouse. Fortunately, he was able to see how his actions were putting his daughter in the middle of this particular conflict with his child's mother and that it was best to discontinue sending her with these messages or child support payments. These kinds of situations can be very explosive if a question or message angers the parent receiving it. An angry response in front of the child can be very destructive, especially if the responding parent further asks the child to relay that response.

Parents often make the mistake of bad-mouthing, belittling, or criticizing the other parent in front of the child (Waldron). This can be very distressing to children, and for many parents, unfortunately, being openly critical of the other parent is one of the most difficult behaviors to contain. Unfortunately, many of us in school-age care see the results of these nasty exchanges between parents in the behaviors of their children. On one occasion, a teacher in my program asked me to take a particular 4th grade child into my office while she called his mother to come pick him up. He had been uncontrollable all day, "bouncing off the walls," as she put it to me. It was when he attempted to run away from her and the group that she knew it was time to call for help. He and I have a pretty good relationship, and I asked him to sit at my assistant's desk and just take a minute to calm down. He was very agitated and jittery. The next thing he did was to take a piece of tape from the tape dispenser, and while trying to place it over his mouth he said to me, "I'm all in pieces. I have to hold myself together." When his mother arrived she related the following to me. The night before, his Dad came to the house to pick him up and had some papers with him that he expected Mom to sign. Instead, Mom told Dad that she would have her lawyer look it over before she would sign it. Dad's response was, in her words, to go "ballistic." He began shouting at her, and, I suppose, she responded in kind. He then put his son in the car and took off. A few minutes later, according to Mom, he turned around and brought their son back to her. Apparently, the child began crying and carrying on in the car and his father couldn't deal with it. The next day, this child was, understandably, "all in pieces."

Many parents who are separating are in a kind of war with their ex-spouses (Trafford, 1982). They are hurt, angry, and grieving and are engaged in hurtful and angry exchanges. They fear the loss of their children or want to hurt their ex-spouses by winning over the children. They try to interfere with the children's natural attachments and prey on their loyalties trying to create an alignment of themselves and the children against the other parent.

> *Criticizing and making derogatory remarks about the other parent*
> *is very damaging to the child. Children identify with both of their*
> *parents; they take on many of their parents' interests and characteristics*
> *as an important part of their developing identity. When a parent denigrates*
> *the other parent, the child experiences this as a direct assault on the*
> *child's own self-esteem. For a child to hear that "Your father is a liar"*
> *or "Your mother is crazy" is to hear "You are a liar" and "You are crazy."*
> *If a child is turned against the other parent, psychologically speaking half*
> *of the child turns against the other half, and there starts an internal war*
> *that can get played out in many ways, all of them destructive.*
>
> *(Waldron, 1995, pp.50-51)*

Parents also make the mistake of using their children as spies—questioning them as to what the other parent is doing, whom the parent is seeing and how the other parent is spending their money. And, conversely, parents will also make the mistake of asking their children to keep secrets from the other parent. This is also very damaging to children and puts them in a very uncomfortable position. Parents who use their children as pawns in the struggle between them have clearly lost sight of the needs of their children to have the right to love both parents. When parents belittle or criticize the other parent to the child or use the children as messengers and spies, it does not serve them well. In fact, it can have just the opposite effect; children often become protective of the other parent and angry with the one who is doing the criticizing and placing them in the middle of the conflict. As one adult child of divorce related when she was placed in this position, "I knew that when my mother was asking me questions about my father, about how he spent his money, it was not out of an interest in me. She was just looking for information, and I would become very protective of my father."

Struggles over the children and struggles over finances play a big part in the conflicts that parents are going through. A devastating mistake parents make is to abandon their children, either physically, emotionally or financially. Failing to maintain child support payments, to keep promises, to follow through on commitments, to maintain regular and consistent contact with the children can all have damaging effects on the children. Or one parent may try to deny access of the other parent to the child. For example, if Dad hasn't paid child support on time Mom won't allow him to see the children or will make visitation or access difficult in

What Parents Can Do

❖ Remember that children need to love BOTH parents.

❖ Be patient and honest – keeping in mind what is appropriate to the age of the children.

❖ Parents need to take care of themselves and their own well-being.

❖ Reassure their children that they will always be their parent.

❖ Reassure children that the divorce is an adult problem. They did NOT cause it.

❖ Allow children to express their feelings.

❖ Offer comfort, warmth and support.

❖ Make significant adults in the children's lives aware of the divorce. (school, child care, etc.)

other more subtle ways. Children experiencing the separation of their parents already have a fear of abandonment, therefore, children need their parents' reassurance that they will not go away from them. An extreme example of how a child's fear of abandonment can manifest itself occurred during a parent education class I taught. The class was from 7:00 to 10:00 PM and met twice a month. A mother came to this evening class with her ten-year-old son. He stayed in the waiting room throughout both sessions. She told us that he would not let her out of his sight, and bringing him with her was the only way she could participate. She had to be with him always or he would get extremely upset and agitated. She even had to accompany him to school or he would not go. His father had left the family and was living with the children's former nanny. It's impossible to know all the details and reasons for this child's behavior, but it was clear that he was very insecure and feared he might lose his mother if he wasn't with her every minute of the day and night.

School-age care providers and youth care specialists are placed in the awkward position of being witnesses to the bad behaviors of parents going through difficult divorces and seeing the effects on the children. Even more troubling is the fact that parents not only place the children in the middle of their conflicts, but also attempt to place their children's caregivers in the middle as well. All of these factors have a profound effect on the ability of school-age care providers and youth care specialists to meet the needs of the children and families in their programs.

Chapter Four:
Implications and Applications to the Field of School-Age Care

*All children experience trauma from parental divorce.
It cannot be avoided, but can be diminished...*
(Erickson & Erickson, 1992)

The number of marriages ending in divorce, although alarmingly high, has in fact declined about 10% over the past ten years (Waldron, 1995). However, it still remains that, at the very least, one third to one fourth of marriages end in divorce and approximately one million children experience parental separation every year (National Center for Health Statistics, 1994 & 1995). This has strong implications for all who work with school-age children. It is, in fact, now a part of life for many children and families, and although school-age children may not be alone in their situations, they are each feeling the painful effects of their parent's separation and no amount of "safety in numbers" can diminish their own unique reactions.

People and programs providing care to school-age children can follow some specific steps in order to adequately meet the particular needs of the children and families they serve who are experiencing divorce and separation. The first step is to identify the issues that arise with children and families that are directly related to divorce and separation and which impact all involved: the children, their parents and the SAC staff. The next step is to develop and define written policies to address these issues in order that parents and program staff are clear about the procedures and expectations in matters of divorce and separation. And, finally, program staff should learn about the issues; examine their own feelings about marriage, family, divorce and separation; and receive training on how to respond and be of support to the families they serve.

STEP ONE: Identifying the Issues: Children's Behaviors, Parent Behaviors and the Role of the School-Age Care Provider

The first step for providers is to look at the individuals in your own programs. Identify the particular issues that you are dealing with as they directly relate to the parents and children in your care. These issues will involve dealing with and responding to children's behaviors as the children try to navigate through their parents' separation and divorce. The children's fears, their anger, their worries, their sadness and depression, are with them when they attend SAC programs. They may verbalize their worries, be overly sensitive and cry easily or withdraw and isolate themselves from others. Or they may act out angry feelings by getting into arguments and conflicts with their peers or by being disrespectful, belligerent and argumentative with the program staff.

The parental issues for caregivers involve the parents' behavior, especially when it is the parents, themselves, who are impacting their children in negative ways by making the kinds of mistakes discussed in the previous chapter. If we accept that parents are the most important people in a child's life, it follows, then, that if they are having difficulties handling the divorce and separation it will directly effect their children's ability to cope. For school-age care providers and youth care specialists this presents a particular challenge, not only in their role of caregiver for the children, but in their interactions with the children's parents. Parents who are in need of support and guidance may look to the caregiver for advice. This in and of itself is not necessarily a problem as most parents have the best interests of their children first and foremost in their minds and only want to do what's best for them. However, the danger lies in situations when the parent, rather than seeking unbiased advice, is really looking for an ally in the battle with their ex-spouse and wants the caregiver to take sides.

There are many concerns that school-age care providers and youth care specialists have expressed and identified in regard to children of divorce. However, two main concerns have emerged with local program staff and others across the country, and from participants at training conferences. The first is their concern about parents who speak negatively about the other parent to them and in front of their children. The second is the concern about parents who ask them to take sides in the battle.

> *There's a lot of game playing back and forth...I don't like being put in the middle; one parent will make remarks about the other parent. The children also make remarks about what one parent has said about the other parent.*
>
> (related by a family child care provider)

Another provider remarked that, "The main thing that is difficult for me to deal with is when the parents are engaged in a tug-of-war over the child, each bad mouthing the other, and the child is caught in the middle. ...If there is a custody issue, ...it is scary to think of denying a parent access to a child." The situations these respondents describe are not unusual. They are, in fact, typical of the actions and behaviors of many parents experiencing difficult divorces.

Completing the first step involves defining the role of the school-age care provider and youth care specialist in dealing with the concerns that children and families of divorce bring into their lives. First and foremost, it is the role of providers to develop positive and supportive relationships with the families they serve. If it is accepted that the caregiver's role is to provide an atmosphere which fosters positive development in children and that caregivers have become, in effect, the "new extended family," then that becomes the base from which all actions stem. In this capacity, school-age care providers and youth care specialists have the ability and the responsibility to make a positive difference in children's lives. As one program director put it, "Providing a support system, referrals and assistance for parents is an important part of [the] SAC provider's relationship with the family." However, we must be careful to approach this responsibility in an appropriate manner. In respect to the children and families of divorce, this means keeping a neutral position while maintaining the delicate balance of being helpful without being intrusive.

The challenge to school-age care providers lies in how to respond to the concerns and behaviors of the parents in order to be supportive without being judgmental. One way in which programs can, in effect, equip themselves to address these concerns is through written policies.

STEP TWO: Develop a Written Policy

A program that has strong policies about most aspects of its operation has a strong foundation from which to handle issues as they arise. While most programs have policies for payment of fees; attendance and enrollment requirements; the days and hours of operation; behavior policies; program philosophy; staff requirements and development, etc., few programs have specific written policies on the issues of children of divorce. One program director connected to the military reported excellent procedures for referrals to support systems within the military and in their schools and community. Other programs reported loose guidelines, such as, "We try to stay neutral," but most providers echo what one said, "We have no written policy, we do what we are legally bound to do in cases of custody. ...We treat each case as it comes along and do our best to provide a safe and nurturing place for children to be."

As illustrated by the actual experiences of school-age program staff, it is clear that children and families of divorce create issues that are uniquely due to the divorce situation. Therefore, policies that are specific to the issues of divorce are needed. For instance, what would be your policy if one parent tells you not to allow the other parent to pick up their child at your program? How do you respond when one parent tells you that they are not responsible to pay for child care? As one program director described, "There was a family that were bitterly at odds with each other over custody, etc. Mom was not getting support from Dad...[and] insisted that her ex-husband was responsible [for the child care payments]. Dad said he just didn't have the money. We were in the middle of a very uncomfortable situation." What can you do when one parent is badmouthing or complaining to you about the other parent in front of the children? How do you respond when a parent's significant other demands behavior reports on the children in an attempt to gather information to be used as ammunition against the children's other parent?

Programs would be well served if written policies were developed that addressed these concerns. Written policies and guidelines will help program staff remain neutral and respond in appropriate ways to the issues that arise. To address the above mentioned concerns as well as others that may arise, here are some suggested guidelines to draw upon for a program policy which relates specifically to children and families of divorce:

1. The written policy should reflect the program's philosophy and might begin with a simple statement such as:

> *It is the mission of the XYZ Program to be a support to families and to promote positive development for children. We recognize that many families are in transition and have experienced divorce and separation. In order to provide the best possible care for your child, who is our main priority, we feel that it is vitally important that we be able to maintain good relations with all the significant adults in his/her life.*

2. The policy statement should clearly outline what parents can expect from you and what you expect from them, i.e.:

> *The staff of the XYZ Program are trained in and sensitive to the issues of divorce and separation. The Executive Director/Administrator of the program asks that you make an appointment to meet privately with him/her and the Site Director in order to discuss any matters of importance in relation to the divorce/separation and any other issues that may help us in the care of your child. For instance, we need to be very clear in regard to the following:*

✔ what the custody arrangements are;

✔ which parent to contact first for general questions and in an emergency;

✔ whether duplicate program information should be sent to both parents;

✔ who is responsible for payments to the XYZ Program;

✔ who will or will not be authorized to pick up the children;

✔ which parent will pick up the child on which days;

✔ who the other significant adults are in the child's life and their relationship to the child, especially if we are to have contact with them as well;

✔ it will also be helpful to discuss the child's general feelings as you see it so we may be appropriately responsive to your child when he/she is with us.

Enrollment forms may cover most, if not all, of the above information. In our program, I have developed a separate form that directly asks the above questions of parents who are divorced or divorcing. This form is filled out at the time of enrollment or if their circumstances change during the year. However, meeting personally with one or both parents will provide an early means to establishing a good relationship with the family and may bring out issues and concerns that are hard to glean from answers to questions on forms.

3. It is important also to state parent-behavior issues clearly in written-policy guidelines. A stated policy can minimize situations that play out parental conflicts in front of the children at the program, i.e.:

In an effort to minimize situations which may be uncomfortable for you, your child and our staff, we ask that parents refrain from talking about custody issues, visitation disputes and problems with, or talking negatively about, the child's other parent in front of the children. Please note, we cannot deny a parent access to their child upon the word of the other parent unless we have a copy of a court order stating that this is the case. If there are concerns of which we need to be aware, please arrange to meet privately with the Site Director and/or Administrator. Once again, it is the child's well being that is our main priority and we need to be able to maintain good relations with both parents.

Written policies for parents are very important as they can facilitate the handling of many situations with parents as they arise and may even provide a means of avoiding difficult situations before they happen. But written policies are just one piece of the equation.

STEP THREE: The Program Staff

The people in a child's life are an important factor in helping them cope with their parents' divorce and separation. Obviously, to the child, the parent is the most important person in the world. Yet, while that child is in the school-age care program it is the staff who can make a difference and who have the opportunity to be a positive influence and support to the child's growth and development. Staff can help children experience parental divorce and separation in positive ways and be responsive to parents in a manner that is sensitive and appropriate.

There are many scenarios that may be played out in front of staff either directly or indirectly. They may witness behaviors of children and parents while at the program or they may hear "stories" related to them by the parent or child. Staff may also become aware of situations by being contacted directly by the courts or from the school or other children's agencies in the community. And, staff may hear about situations just by being a member of the same community as the families they serve. It is, therefore, vitally important that families can trust the program staff and administrators to maintain confidentiality and to refrain from being a source of information (gossip) about the families and children they serve. It is also very important that staff understand that people going through divorce and separation experience changes beyond their control and are enmeshed in conflicts beyond their experiences. This understanding is not to provide an excuse for parents behaving badly, but to provide staff with a context to draw from and explains the conflicts with which parents may be struggling.

When two people separate they are thrown into a whole range of conflicting emotions about themselves and about each other. There is guilt, anger, sadness and confusion. The dynamics have completely changed and they must learn a whole new way of dealing with each other. Two people who have lived together for many years no longer trust one another, have difficulty communicating in a civil manner, emotions are high and they may even feel as if they hate each other. Parents who are distrustful, resentful and angry with one another do not always act in their child's best interest, but act, instead, in ways that are designed to get back at the other parent, sometimes at the expense of their children, or worse, by using their children. One situation was related about a six-year-old child who was "held hostage" by his father from his mother over money issues. "The mother …filed a bench warrant against the father for not paying child support. When the father had his son for a visit, he retaliated by refusing to give back his son to the mother until the mother stopped the bench warrant. The child lost a day of school over this incident."

Program staff often have to face issues due to parental divorce unlike any other issues they may face. One issue that can arise, but is not often openly talked about, is the divorcing or newly single parent's sexuality. Rarely, if ever, would a school-age care provider or youth care specialist have a conversation about personal sexual matters with the married parents of children in their programs. However, the newly single parents of divorce may very well talk about boyfriends, girlfriends or dating experiences to program staff and many will have significant others authorized to pick-up their children.

One director mentioned how parents following a divorce are emotionally needy and may look to the child care provider for comfort. She related a situation she encountered that illustrates how the single-parent relationships with school-age program staff might change:

> *[A recently divorced father of one of the children] took my interest for the well-being of their family for something more. He was very vulnerable…. He showed more interest but I paid it no attention. [His daughter] was now starting to make hints that her father was interested in me. She seemed happy with this selection because I think she realized that he would start dating and I was someone she liked. …I thought the best way to deal with this situation was to carry on as usual. It worked and eventually the situation subsided. The father found someone [else] to date.*

These issues as well as others that program staff face must be handled in ways that are responsible and appropriate and, at the same time, caring and sensitive to the families involved.

Another concern voiced by colleagues and the staff at my own program is that as a result of divorce one parent may become overprotective or over-reactive, "They are very concerned about their children's adjustment and that makes me hesitate to bring up minor trials that they may blow out of proportion." Hesitancy to involve parents in the care of their children at the program stems from a worry that the parent will over-react.

> *[One recently divorced mother went along on a field trip.] This mom was on top of her son all day, correcting, reprimanding, lecturing, cajoling, henpecking to the point where the boy just broke out in tears. Later, when she and I talked, she revealed to me that she was terrified that her son would grow up immoral because her ex-husband was living "in sin" with another woman and that this would have a tremendous impact on her son.*

Some parents may become overly protective, but others may pull away from their children as illustrated by another director who explains:

> *Many of the single parents are very tired and have very little tolerance for the children – especially after working all day. There is very little reprieve for them once they get out of work and begin dinner. From my experience, the parents lose interest in helping with the child's homework and become less involved in the school community as a whole. My single parents are also more depressed and talk about being overwhelmed.*

How, then, do we help the children who are having a rough time dealing with their parents' separation? What is our response when a child expresses fear that he may never see his father again or that his mother spends all her time working or with her own friends and has no time for him? Or the child who worries that she may be replaced by the children of Mommy or Daddy's new friend? One person described a ten-year-old boy who "started losing his hair in patches due to his emotional state as his parents were divorcing." Another described a seven-year-old child who is "often confused as to who will pick him up on rotating Fridays – [he becomes] very tense during program time." And, then there was the eight-year-old girl who "still panics if Mom does not meet her after school. [She] wanted to stop coming to the program after school (and didn't want to go to school). [They] found out that the mother was constantly threatening the child if she misbehaved that she would not be home when she returned from school and that she may never come back for her. The mother told [them] that this was the only way she could get her daughter to listen to her." Fortunately, the caregiver was able to convince the mother to enroll in parenting classes for divorcing families and reported that things were better one year later. As she went on to suggest, "Counseling and support is critical even to the seemingly adjusted children and families."

The above scenarios illustrate the wide variety of issues and concerns that arise with children and families due to their experiences through separation and divorce. Staff training is an important component in preparing one to be able to appropriately respond to the needs of children and families.

To facilitate staff training and discussions on the topic of children of divorce, I repeat an exercise I use with parents in the parent education class. I ask staff to reflect back on their own childhood and try to imagine how they might have felt if their own parents had come to them with the news that they were separating and divorcing. This can be painful for some staff, because they may have actually experienced their parents' divorce, but others may think it is inconceivable that their parents would have contemplated divorce or would ever divorce. I remind them that to most children it is inconceivable to them, too. This exercise helps staff to personalize, somewhat, the emotions and reactions children may be experiencing by putting themselves in the children's "shoes" for a moment of reflection.

One note of caution, however, involves staff who may bring their own preconceived notions and possible prejudices in how they respond to children and families. For example, a person may have deeply held convictions that cause them to view any family of divorce in a negative way and may feel that marriages are sacred and vows are not to be broken. A person with these feelings may have little tolerance for parents who are divorced and may make inappropriate comments about their feelings on the subject or may inappropriately encourage couples to get back together or encourage children's fantasies who are wishing their parents would reunite. There are also staff members who may feel that they are very tolerant of all family situations, but staff can make some mistakes, too. Staff may allow themselves to take sides in the parents' battle, may feel that one parent is more to blame than the other is, and may not see the harm in commiserating with one parent against the other. Allowing staff to express their point of view is important. However, it is most important that all staff recognize the importance of remaining neutral, of keeping their personal feelings to themselves and focusing on the child's well-being. This concern can, of course, be addressed through staff training that can sensitize and educate staff on the many issues that children and families face and how they can be helpful in meaningful ways.

Developing "What to do if…" scenarios and situations can help staff prepare and, perhaps, be able to forestall many uncomfortable situations. You can develop situational scenarios based on the actual experiences you may be having with the children, parents and staff in your own programs. For example, the following two sample questions illustrate how staff might respond based on the program's policy.

> 1. *What would you do if confronted by a parent of divorce at the time of pick-up with a barrage of complaints about the other parent?*

One response might be:

> Staff quickly and gently redirect the parent away from earshot of the children and say to the parent that "I can understand that you are feeling upset and angry, but it is best (and it is the program's policy) that we talk about these issues away from the children."

What Staff Can Do

Staff can:

- ➡ encourage children to express their feelings

- ➡ provide opportunities for children to exercise personal control

- ➡ teach children coping skills and encourage artwork or physical activities such as sports or hobbies that provide healthy outlets for their feelings

- ➡ encourage parents to avoid talking to children about adult problems

- ➡ encourage parents to seek professional help for their children (and themselves) if needed

- ➡ provide tolerant, calming and kind words and be good listeners, patient, compassionate and loving

Staff should:

- ➡ establish clear expectations for children in regard to program rules and behavior

- ➡ avoid being drawn into the parent's conflict

- ➡ keep parents informed of their children's behavior and performance in a supportive manner

- ➡ be aware of the warning signs of depression and fears

2. What would you do if a parent pumps you for information to use against the other parent? Or asks for a detailed accounting of the other parent's payments or pick-up times (i.e., how often late, how often does someone else pick up)?

One response might be:
> "This request puts us in an uncomfortable position with the other parent. Therefore, the information requested can only be released with the consent of both parents or by court order." Staff can remind the parent of the program's policy and the need for staff to maintain good relationships with both parents as well as all the significant adults in the child's life.

Through maintaining good relations with both parents one is more likely to come to agreement and avoid repeating unpleasant scenarios. Once again, it is the child's well-being that is the priority.

The school-age care provider and youth care specialist can make a difference and have a positive effect in helping children of divorce. Here are some specific suggestions on what program staff can do for the children in their care whose parents are going through a divorce:

❖ Staff can *encourage children to express their feelings*, to talk about the divorce with them or with their parents or a relative, friend or teacher they trust. Children want their caregivers, parents and teachers to listen and talk with them about their feelings.

❖ Staff can *provide opportunities for children to exercise personal control* over meaningful activities, procedures and events since children experiencing their parents' divorce have virtually no control over many divorce related events. This lack of control may threaten a child's developing sense of mastery. Assigning leadership roles to children of divorce which lead to successful outcomes can help improve a child's self image.

❖ Staff can *teach children coping skills and encourage artwork or physical activities such as sports or hobbies that provide healthy outlets for their feelings.*

❖ Staff should *establish clear expectations for children in regard to program rules and behavior.*

❖ Staff should *avoid being drawn into the parent's conflict* and not take sides or support one parent's claims over the other.

❖ Staff can *encourage parents to avoid talking to children about adult problems* and to make every effort to give children the sense that everything will work out well and that their world is secure.

❖ Staff should *keep parents informed of their children's behavior and performance in a supportive manner.*

❖ Staff should *be aware of the warning signs of depression and fears.*

❖ Staff can *encourage parents to seek professional help for their children (and themselves) if needed.*

❖ And, most importantly, staff can *provide tolerant, calming and kind words and be good listeners, patient, compassionate and loving.*

Finally, program administrators and staff can develop a resource list for parents of books, articles, professional counselors, agencies, parenting classes and support groups available to parents and children experiencing divorce and separation. The school district also may have resources to which the after-school program can refer the family

The military has a standing operating procedure that includes referrals to the special needs coordinator, health professionals and family counselors. These individuals work with the SAC staff on a regular basis and have formed a team which meets monthly to review cases and address concerns about children. They also have a referral system for the parents which includes family and community resources, financial assistance programs, alcohol and substance abuse programs, counseling services and housing assistance. We still need to work on more financial assistance for parents, low cost care and low cost housing. We have made progress in these areas but that is one reason that we are working on collaborating with the YMCA, 4-H Clubs and Boys and Girls Clubs to provide more low-cost or free care options for parents. These options combined with our SAC program and academic after-school programs provided by the schools offer the parent more variety of choices to meet their needs.

(related by a director of an Army-based school-age program)

Parents need support on many levels and in places that may not be immediately apparent. School-age programs can link people to places and services that may be able to provide families with the support they need. School-age programs that develop a list of the available supports in their area are providing a valuable service to the families in their program.

Chapter Five:
Concluding Thoughts

Children of divorce attending school-age programs bring with them a whole range of behaviors, feelings and emotions. School-age care providers and youth care specialists can make a positive difference by being responsive, support-ive and knowledgeable in helping the children and their families through the adjust-ments of going through divorce and separation. However, we might ask ourselves, how is this different from all children who come from a wide range of backgrounds and family situations? What we know from the research and literature on children of divorce can certainly be applied to any child experiencing loss in their lives and to any child who may be experiencing parental conflict in the home. Conversely, what we may know from other resources that teach and train us in conflict resolu-tion, problem solving, communication skills with children and parents, child devel-opment, health and safety practices, group dynamics, planning appropriate activi-ties, etc. can, of course, be applied to dealing with children of divorce. Therefore, school-age care providers and youth care specialists must rely on their good judg-ment and common sense coupled with a foundation of experience, practice and knowledge which is necessary to enhance these qualities.

In all situations there are a wealth of resources within reach for making a posi-tive impact on the children in school-age care. The first step is to learn how divorce and separation affect children and families. Learning how children respond and why they may be feeling the way they do according to their particular situation and developmental stage can provide a knowledge base for staff in responding appropri-ately to children and assisting parents in the process. Learning the warning signs in children and the common mistakes parents make will allow staff to offer parents assistance in getting professional help for themselves or their children before problems persist. And, most importantly, addressing the issues head-on, with clearly written policies and staff training will provide a means to avoid uncomfort-able situations for children, parents and staff, hopefully before they begin.

Finally, providing resources to families is another way of being supportive in a meaningful manner. Sources for services to divorcing parents can come from the schools, family service agencies, mental health agencies, child guidance clinics, private mental health professionals, family doctors, ministers, priests and rabbis. In addition to finding the agencies and outside programs in their local areas that provide support for families and children going through divorce and separation, program administrators and staff can keep a library of books, pamphlets, and magazine articles on the subject, or offer the families a list of these resources. The bibliography at the end of this book includes a number of titles that would be useful to both parents and children.

The Internet is a wonderful resource and has many sites devoted to divorce for parents and children that can be helpful. Websites that parents can be referred to, plus websites that will be helpful to the school-age care provider are listed below.

In many states, parent education courses are available to parents who are separating and divorcing. For parents who take these courses early on in the process of divorcing, the course has a beneficial effect on improving communication between ex-spouses and increasing the willingness of parents to seek further services to help with their adjustments to the divorce. Much of the information in this book comes from the materials designed for the parent education course I teach as they are directly related to easing the trauma for children experiencing parental separation and divorce.

Program administrators and staff can make a difference for children and families of divorce by becoming informed of the issues and being valuable resources for parents and children. By developing positive, supportive and trusting relationships with the families they serve they can comfortably make referrals when necessary to parents who may need professional counseling or whose children may be in need of outside resources. Having clearly written policies, early discussions with parents, and staff training on how to handle and address the issues of divorce will help all involved to work together to meet the needs of the children and families in school-age care programs, enhancing the quality of care for the children and helping further the role of school-age care providers and youth care specialists as the *new extended family*.

Online Resources

(Please note: this information was current at the time of publication.)

www.divorce-online.com

www.divorcesource.com

www.divorcewizards.com

Academy of Child & Adolescent Psychiatry: **www.aacap.org**

For caregivers and providers the National Network for Child Care's web pages has helpful information: **www.nncc.org**

References

Adler, A., & Archambault, C. (1990). *Divorce recovery: Healing the hurt through self-help and professional support.* Washington, D.C.: The PIA Press.

Academy of Child & Adolescent Psychiatry (February, 1999). *AACAP Facts for Families*, Fact No.1 (Updated 8/98). (http://www.aacap.org/factsFam/divorce.htm).

Baris, M., & Garrity, C. (1988). *Children of divorce: A developmental approach to residence and visitation.* DeKalb, IL: Psytec Corporation.

Bradburn-Stern, B. (1990). *Children cope with divorce: Trainer's manual.* Atlanta, GA: Families First.

DeBord, Karen. (1999). *The effects of divorce on children.* National Network for Child Care. Retrieved January 18, 1999 from the World Wide Web: http://www.nncc.org/Child.Dev/ effectsdivorce.html.

Divorce Online (Sept. 1997, Jan. 1999). (http://www.divorce-online.com).

Divorce Source (Jan. 1999). (http://www.divorcesource.com).

Divorce Wizards (Feb. 1999). (http://www.divorcewizards.com).

Elkind, D. (1994). *The ties that stress: The new family imbalance.* Cambridge, MA: Harvard University Press.

Erickson, M., & Erickson, S. (1992). *The children's book: ...for the sake of the children.* West Concord, MN: CPI Publishing.

Geasler, M. J., & Blaisure, K. R. (1998). *A review of divorce education program materials.* Family Relations. Vol. 47, No. 2. pp. 167-175.

Grusec, J., & Lytton, H. (1988). *Social development: History, theory, and research.* New York, NY: Springer-Verlag.

Keller, Bess (1997, April 9). *Divorce increasingly puts schools in the middle of family conflicts* [Abstract]. Education Week v. 16. P. 1+il. Retrieved November 8, 1997 from telnet.columbianet.cc.columbia.edu.

Kendall, E.D., et al. (May, 1981). *Effects of changed family structures on children: A review of the literature.* [Abstract]. Information analysis. 63p. Retrieved November 8, 1997 from telnet.columbianet.cc.columbia.edu.

Kubler-Ross, E. (1969). *On death and dying.* New York, NY: Macmillan Publishing Co., Inc.

Lansky, V. (1989). *Vicki Lansky's Divorce book for parents: Helping your children cope with divorce and its aftermath.* New York, NY: Signet.

Marston, S. (1994). *The divorced parent.* New York, NY: Wm. Morrow & Co.

Miller, P., Ryan, P., and Morrison, W. (1999). *Practical strategies for helping children of divorce in today's classroom.* Childhood Education: Infancy Through Early Adolescence. Annual Theme 1999, v. 75, no. 5, pp. 285-289

National Center for Health Statistics (Release April 18, 1995) *Highlights of a new report from the national center for health statistics (NCHS)*: Advance report of final divorce statistics, 1989 and 1990. Monthly Vital Statistics Report, Vol. 43, No. 9 Supplement.

National Center for Health Statistics (1994) *Annual summary of births, marriages, divorces, and deaths: United States, 1994.*

National Center for Health Statistics (1998) *Fastats, A to Z, Statistical Rolodex: Divorce. Monthly Vital Statistics Report,* Vol. 45, No 12.

Oesterreich, Lesia. (1999). *Divorce matters: A child's view.* National Network for Child Care

Ollhoff, J. & Ollhoff, L. (1996). *School-age care providers: Extended day or extended family?: A staff development book.* MN Department of Children, Families, and Learning, SACC Initiative.

Trafford, A. (1982). *Crazy time: Surviving divorce.* New York, NY: Bantam Books.

U.S. Census Bureau (1995) *Living arrangements of children under 18 years old: 1960 to the present.*

Waldron, K.H. (1995). *Children of divorce: an educational program for divorcing parents – understanding the dual divorce.* 2nd Edition. Madison, WI: Kenneth H. Waldron, Ph.D. Founding Director, Custody Counseling Project, Capital Square Associates.

Wallerstein, J. & Kelly, J. (1980). *Surviving the breakup: How children and parents cope with divorce.* New York, NY: Basic Books, Inc.

Bibliography

Berger, T. (1976). *How does it feel when your parents get divorced?* New York, NY: Messner.

Blau (Blaw), M. (1995). *Families apart: Ten keys to successful co-parenting.* New York, NY: Perigee, a division of The Berkeley Publishing Group.

Blue, R. (1972). *A month of sundays.* New York, NY: Watts.

Blume, J. (1986). *It's not the end of the world.* New York, NY: Bradbury Press

Boegehold, B. (1985). *Daddy doesn't live here anymore.* Wisconsin: Western Publishing.

Bonkowski, S. (1987). *Kids are non-divorceable: A workbook for divorced parents and their children,* Ages 6-11 version. Chicago, IL: Buckley Publications.

Booher, D. (1979). *Coping when your family falls apart.* New York, NY: Messner.

Brown, L., & Brown, M. (1986). *The dinosaurs divorce.* New York, NY: Little Brown & Co.

Ciborowski, P. J., (1988). *Survival skills for single parents!* Port Chester, NY: Stratmar Educational Systems.

Ciborowski, P. J., Chairman, American Mental Health Counselors Association Committee on Childhood & Adolescence. (No date). *Helping children cope with separation and divorce: A resource pamphlet for parents, educators and mental health professionals.* Port Chester, NY: Stratmar Educational Systems.

Cleary, B. (1984). *Dear mr. henshaw.* New York, NY: Dell.

Franke, L. (1983). *Growing up divorced.* New York, NY: Simon & Schuster.

Friedman, J. (1984). *The divorce handbook: Your basic guide to divorce.* Updated. New York, NY: Random House, Inc.

Galper, M. (1980). *Joint custody and co-parenting: Sharing your child equally.* New York, NY: Running Press.

Gardner, R. (1971). *The boys and girls book about divorce.* New York, NY: Bantam Books.

Gardner, R. (1979). *The parents' book about divorce.* New York, NY: Bantam Books.

Goff, B. (1969). *Where is daddy? The story of divorce.* Boston, MA: Beacon Press.

Grollman, E. (1969). *Explaining divorce to children.* Boston, MA: Beacon Press.

Grollman, E. (1975). *Talking about divorce.* Boston, MA: Beacon Press.

Hickey, E., & Dalton, E. (1994). *Healing hearts: Helping children and adults recover from divorce.* Carson City, NV: Gold Leaf Press.

Kalter, N. (1990). *Growing up with divorce: Helping your child avoid immediate and later emotional problems.* New York, NY: Macmillan Publishing Co.

Krantzler, M. (1974). *The creative divorce.* New York, NY: Signet.

Krementz, J. (1984). *How it feels when your parents divorce.* New York, NY: Knopf.

LeShan, E. (1978). *What's going to happen to me?* New York, NY: Four Winds Press.

Mayle, Peter (1988). *Divorce can happen to the nicest people.* New York, NY: Harmony.

Ricci, I. (1997). *Mom's house, dad's house — making shared custody work.* 2nd Edition. New York, NY: Collier Books, Macmillan Publishing Co.

Sinberg, J. (1978). *Divorce is a grown-up problem.* New York, NY: Avon Press.

Teyber, E. (1985). *Helping your children with divorce: A comprehensive guide for parents.* New York, NY: Pocket Books.

Thomas, M. (1987). *Free to be...a family.* New York, NY: Bantam Books.

Walther, A. (1991). *Divorce hangover – A step-by-step prescription for creating a bright future after your marriage ends.* New York, NY: Pocket Books a division of Simon & Schuster.

Ware, C. (1984). *Sharing parenthood after divorce: An enlightened custody guide for mothers, fathers and children.* New York, NY: Bantam Books.

Reproducibles

For staff training or presentations on the material contained within this book, the following pages may be copied in multiple quantities as handouts or as transparencies for use with an overhead projector.

FACTS

❖ 1 out of every 3 couples marrying this year will be divorced in 10 years.

❖ 60% of divorces occur for people between the ages of 25-39.

❖ Over 1,000,000 children are affected by divorce each year.

❖ 70% of all children born since 1990 will spend time in a single parent family.

NORMAL REACTIONS
(*Mourning the Marriage*)

In Children

- ❖ Health/Sleep Changes

- ❖ Regression

- ❖ Insecurity

- ❖ Guilt/Self Blame

- ❖ Protective of Parents

In Children & Parents

- ❖ Denial

- ❖ Anger

- ❖ Bargaining

- ❖ Sadness/Depression

- ❖ Acceptance

WHAT KIDS NEED TO DO

❖ Overcome sense of:
    Rejection
    Humiliation
    Unloveableness
    Powerlessness

❖ Resolve Anger

❖ Stop Blaming

❖ Disengage from the Parental Conflict

❖ Accept Reality & Permanence

❖ Preserve Ideals of Love and Loyalty

Warning Signs In Children

- ❖ An exaggeration in the normal responses
- ❖ Frequent nightmares
- ❖ Intense, unrealistic fears
- ❖ Ongoing health complaints
    (i.e., headache, stomachaches, diarrhea, constipation)
- ❖ Extended changes in sleeping or eating habits
- ❖ Preoccupation with illness in self and/or others
- ❖ School troubles, lying, stealing
- ❖ Explosive behavior
- ❖ Accident proneness
- ❖ Verbalizing despair
- ❖ Giving away their possessions
- ❖ Withdrawing to the point of isolation
- ❖ Significant weight loss or gain
- ❖ Destroying own or other's property
- ❖ Deliberately hurting or wounding themselves
- ❖ Significant change in personality
- ❖ Refusing to stay with formerly trusted adults
- ❖ Running away from home or child care setting

The "Don'ts"
Mistakes Parents Make

❖ Sending messages through the children to each other

❖ Asking children to keep secrets from the other parent

❖ Using children as pawns in the power struggle

❖ Belittle and criticize the other parent in front of the children

❖ Telling their children what to think and feel

❖ Asking children to take sides

❖ Become less available to their children emotionally and physically

❖ Pumping their children for information about their ex-spouse

❖ Use children as confidants

❖ Comparing their feelings about their ex or the divorce to those their children have

❖ Putting children in the middle of the parent's conflict

❖ Relying on their children as a source for their own emotional support

What Parents Can Do

❖ Remember that children need to love BOTH parents.

❖ Be patient and honest – keeping in mind what is appropriate to the age of the children.

❖ Parents need to take care of themselves and their own well-being.

❖ Reassure their children that they will always be their parent.

❖ Reassure children that the divorce is an adult problem. They did NOT cause it.

❖ Allow children to express their feelings.

❖ Offer comfort, warmth and support.

❖ Make significant adults in the children's lives aware of the divorce. (school, child care, etc.)